How Far Is Heaven, Mama?

Written by Amy-Lee Campbell
Illustrated by Moli_art

Amy-Lee Campbell
Illustrated by Moli_art

Printed Worldwide
First Printing 2022
First Edition 2022

10 9 8 7 6 5 4 3 2 1

To my five beautiful children.
Dash, Thor, King and their angel sisters in heaven;
Love and Journey.
I am forever grateful for you and
I love you all to infinity and beyond.

~Amy-Lee

This book belongs to:

____

How far is Heaven, Mama?

PLAY
ROOM
COOL

"It's time for bed my little pokaroos!"
Mama says as she enters the room.

COOL

She patiently brushes her children's teeth and gives them each a kiss on the cheek.

The family then climbs into the bed. All looking forward to the books to be read.

When the stories are over Mama begins to pray. Saying Thank you to God for another beautiful day.

cool

They pray for the Earth and all the living things on it. For safety, good health, and the home where they sit.

The last thing they pray is to send their love, to family and friends in heaven above.

With mighty curiosity, Beau who was seven, says "Please tell me Mama, how far is heaven?"

Quickly sweet Thory wanted to guess, he thought his answer would be the best. "Heaven is on the other side of the moon!! Do you think that we could go there soon?

Now baby Ling had a plan, to go on trip
with the entire clan.

"Can we travel way up high?! We'll go get our sisters, are they in the sky?"

Mama holds back her tears and calmly sighs. "I'm sorry my son's but heavens not a place we can see with our eyes."

"I've heard it's the most beautiful place, with peace, joy, beauty and all of God's grace."

"How far heaven is I really don't know, it's a special place where only souls can go."

"I know you wish that you and your
sisters could play."

"And Heaven gives us hope you'll surely
will get to one day."

As they all close their eyes and call it a
night, they share a peaceful feeling
everything will be alright.

The End